Goldberg

Pro Wrestler
Bill Goldberg

by Michael Burgan

Reading Consultant:
Dr. Robert Miller
Professor of Special Education
Minnesota State University, Mankato

Capstone
press ®

Mankato, Minnesota

Capstone High-Interest Books are published by Capstone Press
151 Good Counsel Drive, P.O. Box 669, Mankato, Minnesota 56002
www.capstonepress.com

Library of Congress Cataloging-in-Publication Data
Burgan, Michael.
  Goldberg: pro wrestler Bill Goldberg/by Michael Burgan.
  p. cm.—(Pro wrestlers)
  Includes bibliographical references (p. 45) and index.
  ISBN-13: 978-0-7368-0917-7 (hardcover) ISBN-10: 0-7368-0917-1 (hardcover)
  1. Goldberg, Bill, 1966—Juvenile literature. 2. Wrestlers—United States—
Biography—Juvenile literature. [1. Goldberg, Bill, 1966- 2. Wrestlers.] I. Title:
Pro wrestler Bill Goldberg. II. Title. III. Series
GV1196.G65 B87 2002
796.812'092—dc21
[B]   00-013073

Summary: Traces the personal life and career of professional wrestler Bill Goldberg.

Editorial Credits
Angela Kaelberer, editor; Lois Wallentine, product planning editor;
    Timothy Halldin, cover designer and illustrator; Katy Kudela, photo researcher

Photo Credits
Albert L. Ortega, 10, 40
ALLSPORT PHOTOGRAPHY, cover inset (left), 30
AP/Wide World Photos, cover inset (right), 7, 13
Dr. Michael Lano, 4, 25, 26, 29, 32, 35, 36, 39, 42
Jimmy Cribb, 18, 21
Skye Dumoulin, cover, 22
UGA Sports Communications, 15, 16

Capstone Press thanks Dr. Michael Lano, WReaLano@aol.com, for his assistance in
the preparation of this book.

1 2 3 4 5 6 07 06 05 04 03 02

Table of Contents

Chapter 1

WCW Champion

It was July 6, 1998. Bill Goldberg entered the Georgia Dome in Atlanta, Georgia. More than 40,000 people filled the arena's seats.

The fans wanted to see Bill wrestle for the World Championship Wrestling (WCW) World Championship. Bill's opponent was Terry Bollea. He is known as "Hollywood" Hulk Hogan.

Some professional wrestlers are mean to their opponents or the fans during matches. These wrestlers are called "heels." At the time, Hogan was a heel. Wrestling also has heroes. They are called "babyfaces" or "faces." Bill was one of the most popular faces in wrestling.

Bill Goldberg is one of the most popular wrestlers today.

Early in the night, Hogan announced that he would not wrestle Bill as planned. Instead, Hogan wanted Bill to wrestle Scott Hall. Hall and Hogan both belonged to the New World Order (nWo). This group of heels often wrestled together. Bill first had to beat Hall in order to wrestle Hogan.

First Match

During the match, other members of the nWo came out to help Hall. But basketball player Karl Malone and wrestler Page Falkenburg stopped these wrestlers from entering the ring. Falkenburg wrestles as Diamond Dallas Page.

Bill then used one of his signature moves on Hall. Bill's move was the Spear. Bill crouched next to Hall. He thrust his shoulder into Hall's stomach. Hall doubled over. Bill then lifted Hall and threw him to the mat.

Bill then used another signature move called the Jackhammer. Bill picked up Hall and held him over his head. Bill then crashed Hall headfirst into the mat. Bill covered Hall's body as the referee counted to three. Bill was ready to face Hogan for the championship.

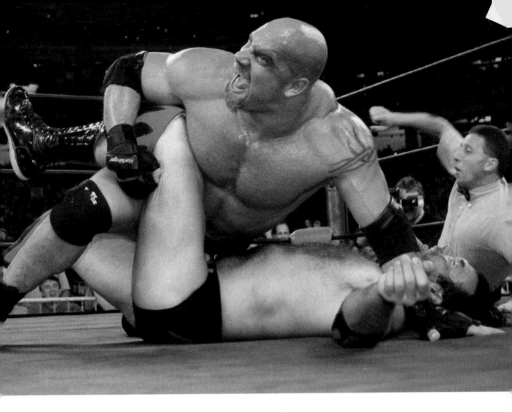

On July 6, 1998, Bill defeated Scott Hall at the Georgia Dome in Atlanta.

Title Match

Bill had only a short rest before his match against Hogan. He began the match by putting Hogan in a headlock. But Hogan escaped. Later, Hogan threw Bill through the ropes and out of the ring. Hogan grabbed a chair and hit Bill with it three times.

Hogan followed Bill back into the ring. Hogan then did a leg drop on Bill. He fell hard on Bill's leg. Hogan looked outside the ring. Karl Malone and wrestler Curt Hennig were fighting outside of the ring. Bill had a chance to get up. He used the Spear on Hogan. He followed the Spear with the Jackhammer. Bill pinned Hogan to the mat. The referee counted to three. Bill was the new World Champion.

About Bill Goldberg

Bill Goldberg is 6 feet 3 inches (191 centimeters) tall and weighs 285 pounds (129 kilograms). He started wrestling in 1997.

Bill began his wrestling career by winning 173 matches in a row. This record is the longest winning streak in modern professional wrestling.

Bill won both the WCW U.S. and World Championship titles during his first year of wrestling. Bill won the U.S. Championship again in 1999. In 1999, he teamed with Bret Hart to win the WCW Tag Team title.

Bill has many interests outside of the ring. He is an actor and has written a book. He also loves animals. He volunteers for the Humane Society of the United States. This group tries to make sure that all animals are treated well. Bill also is proud of his Jewish religion and culture. He is the most successful Jewish wrestler ever.

Major Matches

September 22, 1997—Bill defeats Hugh Morrus to win his first official match.

April 20, 1998—Bill defeats Raven to win the WCW U.S. Championship.

July 6, 1998—Bill defeats "Hollywood" Hulk Hogan to win the WCW World Championship.

December 27, 1998—Bill ends his 173-match winning streak and loses the World Championship to Kevin Nash.

October 24, 1999—Bill defeats Sid Vicious to regain the U.S. Championship.

December 7, 1999—With Bret Hart, Bill defeats Creative Control to win the WCW Tag Team Championship.

December 13, 1999—Bret Hart and Bill lose the Tag Team Championship title to Kevin Nash and Scott Hall.

June 11, 2000—Bill becomes a heel at the Great American Bash. He helps Jeff Jarrett win the WCW World Championship by defeating Kevin Nash.

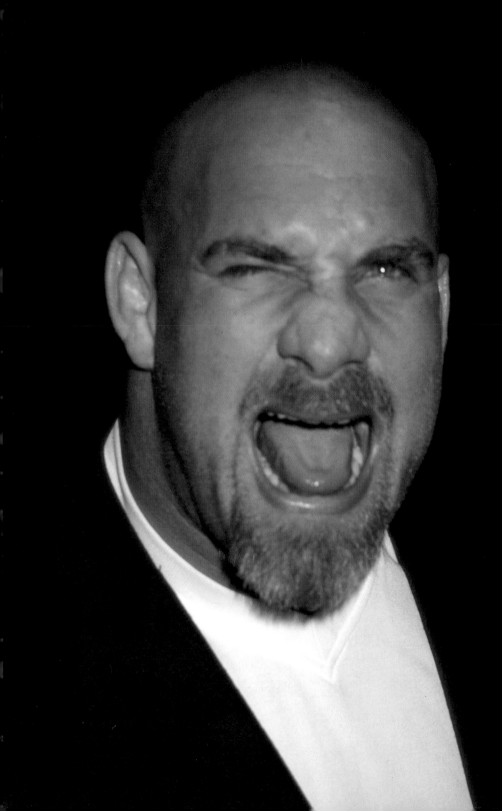

Chapter 2

The Early Years

William Scott Goldberg was born December 27, 1966, in Tulsa, Oklahoma. His parents are Jed and Ethel Goldberg. Jed was a doctor. Ethel was once a professional musician. She played the violin.

Bill is the youngest of four children. He has two brothers. Their names are Mike and Steve. Bill also has a sister named Barbara. Bill's sister and brothers are much older than he is. Mike was 18, Steve was 15, and Barbara was 12 when Bill was born.

Bill was born and grew up in Tulsa, Oklahoma.

A Football Family

Bill grew up watching his brothers play football. In high school, Steve played linebacker. Mike was a defensive lineman. Both Mike and Steve were stars for Thomas Edison High School in Tulsa. They were named among the best high school football players in Oklahoma. Mike and Steve also played football for the University of Minnesota in Minneapolis.

When Bill was 12, Jed and Ethel divorced. The divorce was very difficult for Bill. He played sports to help him through this painful time. He played baseball, basketball, and tennis. But his favorite sport was football. Mike and Steve were Bill's heroes. Bill wanted to be a football player like his brothers.

High School

In high school, Bill was big for his age. He was 6 feet, 3 inches (191 centimeters) tall and weighed 250 pounds (113 kilograms). He was the perfect size for a defensive lineman. He enjoyed playing hard and tackling the other players.

Goldberg's Hero: John Matuszak

John Matuszak was one of Bill's childhood heroes. Matuszak was a defensive lineman for several NFL teams during the 1970s and 1980s. He was the number one pick in the 1973 NFL draft. His best years were with the Oakland Raiders. He helped the Raiders win Super Bowls in 1977 and 1981.

Matuszak was one of the largest football players at the time. He was 6 feet, 8 inches (203 centimeters) tall and weighed 280 pounds (127 kilograms).

Later in his career, Matuszak became an actor. He appeared in movies such as *North Dallas Forty* and on TV shows such as *The A-Team*. Matuszak retired from football in 1982. On June 17, 1989, he died of heart failure. He was 38 years old.

Like his brothers, Bill became a football star at Edison High. Bill was named to Tulsa's All-City team and the Oklahoma All-State team during his last year of high school. He also was named the top defensive player in the state.

In 1985, Bill graduated from Edison High. He accepted a football scholarship from the University of Georgia in Athens. The scholarship paid for Bill's college education. Bill decided to major in psychology at the university. He studied the mind, emotions, and human behavior.

College Star

The University of Georgia sports teams are called the Bulldogs. Bill played defensive tackle for the football team.

The University of Georgia plays in the Southeastern Conference (SEC). Bill was named to the Associated Press All-SEC first team during his third season at Georgia. He led the Bulldogs with 121 tackles.

Bill and the Bulldogs struggled during the 1989 season. The team's record was 6–6. But

In 1985, Bill began classes at the University of Georgia in Athens.

Bill still was named to the All-SEC first team and the All-American second team. He also won the J. B. Whitworth Award. The university gives this award each year to the team's top defensive lineman. Bill had 348 tackles, 178 tackle assists, and 12 sacks during his college football career.

After the season ended, Bill was asked to play in the Japan Bowl with other top college players. National Football League (NFL) teams sent scouts to this game. It was important that Bill play well if he wanted to be drafted by an NFL team. But Bill became sick with mononucleosis two weeks before the game. This illness can cause weakness, a sore throat, and fever. Bill lost 20 pounds (9 kilograms). He did not play well during the game. After this game, some NFL scouts did not think Bill was good enough to play professional football.

Still, the Los Angeles Rams wanted to give Bill a chance. In 1990, the Rams drafted Bill in the 11th round. Bill dropped out of college before receiving his degree. He went to Los Angeles to try out for the Rams.

Bill played defensive tackle for the Bulldogs.

Chapter 3

From Football to Wrestling

The NFL season starts with training camp. Teams practice plays and get into shape at these camps. Coaches also watch the rookies. The coaches decide if these new players are good enough to make the team. Bill practiced and played hard at training camp. But he did not make the team.

The Rams let Bill try out again the next season. Once again, Bill did not make the team. But he was not ready to give up playing football.

Bill wore number 71 when he played for the Atlanta Falcons.

The WLAF

In 1992, Bill had another chance to play professional football. Bill joined the Sacramento Surge in Sacramento, California.

The Surge were part of the World League of American Football (WLAF). This professional league had teams in North America and Europe. The league played during the spring. Many WLAF players hoped to someday play in the NFL.

That season, the Surge beat the Orlando Thunder to win the World Bowl. The Surge were the league champions. Bill was one of the best defensive linemen on the team. NFL scouts again became interested in him. The Atlanta Falcons invited him to their training camp. In summer 1992, Bill returned to Georgia to play for the Falcons.

NFL Career

The Falcons had other defensive linemen who were taller, heavier, and stronger than Bill. He played in only four games in his first season and five in his second season. But Bill was happy to be playing in the NFL.

Bill played two seasons for the Atlanta Falcons.

Injuries kept Bill out of some games. His worst injury came in 1994. The Falcons were playing a preseason game against the Philadelphia Eagles. Bill was hit from behind. A sharp pain shot through his body. The hit tore a muscle near his hip. Bill felt pain whenever he made simple moves. Even getting out of bed was painful.

Bill developed his signature moves after he began his wrestling training.

Bill managed to play in five games that season. But he later learned that the injury was serious. Doctors said he would probably never play football again. But Bill still was not ready to give up on an NFL career.

In 1995, the Carolina Panthers became a new NFL team. The team selected players from other teams. The Panthers picked Bill from the

Falcons. Bill tried to play. But the injury still bothered him. He decided to quit the team. Bill had played football for most of his life. He did not know what to do next.

Becoming a Wrestler

In Atlanta, Bill met wrestlers Steve Borden, Lawrence Pfohl, and Page Falkenburg. These men are known as Sting, Lex Luger, and Diamond Dallas Page. They wrestled for the WCW. At the time, the WCW was based in Atlanta. Bill sometimes trained in a gym owned by Sting and Luger. They convinced Bill to try professional wrestling.

Bill talked to both the WCW and the World Wrestling Federation (WWF) about wrestling for their organizations. The WWF is based in Stamford, Connecticut. Bill wanted to stay in Atlanta. He joined the WCW.

The WCW wanted Bill to train before he wrestled his first match. In early 1996, Bill began training five days each week at the WCW's training center in Atlanta. The training center was called the Power Plant.

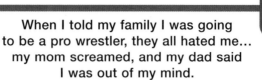

When I told my family I was going
to be a pro wrestler, they all hated me...
my mom screamed, and my dad said
I was out of my mind.
—Bill Goldberg, *Sports Illustrated*, 6/12/00

At the Power Plant, Bill learned many wrestling techniques. He learned how to safely fall to the mat. He also learned how to hit his opponents and take them down to the mat. Bill developed the Spear and the Jackhammer at the Power Plant.

After a few months, Bill was ready for his first match. But first, he had to pick a name. He then had to decide if he would wear a costume or makeup. Most wrestlers develop a character to use when they wrestle. They often wear a costume or use a different name as part of the character. Bill decided to use his own last name. He also chose to wear black wrestling shorts and boots. Bill shaved his head and got a tattoo on his left arm. These changes made him look fierce. Bill was ready to wrestle in the WCW.

Bill shaved his head and got a tattoo before he began wrestling in the WCW.

Chapter 4

WCW Star

Bill wrestled his first match on September 22, 1997. The match took place in Salt Lake City, Utah. Bill faced Bill DeMott. DeMott wrestled as Hugh Morrus. During the match, Bill did a backflip in the ring. He then picked up Morrus and slammed him to the mat. Bill ended the match with the Jackhammer to defeat Morrus.

Bill wrestled often during the next few months. He won all of his matches. Fans began to show an interest in him.

Bill quickly became popular with wrestling fans.

U.S. Champion

On April 20, 1998, Bill had his first chance to wrestle for a championship. He faced Scott Levy for the WCW U.S. Championship. Levy wrestles under the name Raven.

During the match, Peter Gruner, Horace Bollea, and Ron Reis tried to help Raven win. Gruner wrestles as Billy Kidman. Bollea is known as Horace Hogan. Reis wrestles as Reese. These wrestlers were part of a group called Raven's Flock.

Bill threw Kidman out of the ring. He used the Jackhammer on the 400-pound (181-kilogram) Reese. Hogan hit Bill with a stop sign. Bill took the stop sign from Hogan. He then slammed Raven down on the sign. The pin gave Bill the U.S. Championship. It was his 75th win as a professional wrestler.

Victory and Defeat

Bill continued to face some of the best wrestlers in the WCW. On June 13, 1998, he defeated Sting. Sting once had been the WCW

Members of Raven's Flock tried to stop Bill from winning the U.S. Championship.

World Champion. This win prepared Bill for his match against Hulk Hogan. On July 6, Bill defeated Hogan. After the win, Bill then gave up his U.S. Championship. Bill instead wore the World Championship belt.

Bill's winning streak reached 173 matches.

Bill had a busy schedule. He traveled throughout North America. He wrestled four or five times each week. He kept winning.

On August 8, Bill took part in a battle royal in Sturgis, South Dakota. Many wrestlers are in the ring at one time during this type of match. The last wrestler standing is the winner. Bill wrestled against Sting, Curt Hennig, Scott

Norton, Lex Luger, Scott Hall, Kevin Nash, Charles Ashenoff, and Paul Wight. Ashenoff wrestles as Konnan. Wight has wrestled as the Giant and the Big Show. Bill defeated the other wrestlers to win the battle royal.

Bill faced Nash again just a few months later. Bill was still undefeated. He had won 173 matches in a row. On December 27, 1998, Bill met Nash at the MCI Center in Washington, D.C. Bill would defend his World Championship at this match.

In most matches, a wrestler can be disqualified for breaking the rules. The wrestler then loses the match. But this match had no rules. Neither wrestler could be disqualified. Bill and Nash could do anything to win.

During the match, other wrestlers came out to help Nash. Bill drove off the first two wrestlers who tried to attack him. Scott Hall was the third man to try to help Nash. Hall carried a cattle prod. This stick uses electricity to shock animals. Hall used the cattle prod on Bill.

Rival in the Ring: Kevin Nash

Kevin Nash was the first wrestler ever to defeat Bill. Nash is one of the largest wrestlers in the world. He is 7 feet (213 centimeters) tall and weighs about 360 pounds (163 kilograms).

Nash began his career in 1990 with the WCW. In 1993, he moved to the WWF. But he returned to the WCW three years later. He has wrestled under several names during his career. These names include Steel, Oz, Vinnie Vegas, and Diesel. He now uses his own name when he wrestles.

In 1994, Nash won both the WWF World Championship and the WWF Intercontinental title. Nash also is a five-time WCW World Champion. He teamed with Scott Hall to found the New World Order. He and Hall also have wrestled as a tag team called the Outsiders. The Outsiders won the WCW Tag Team title four times.

The cattle prod had tape on it so that Bill would not get seriously hurt. But he still fell to the mat after Hall touched him with the prod. Nash then pinned Bill. Bill lost his first match and the World Championship.

A New Year

In 1999, Bill remained one of the WCW's most popular wrestlers. He won most of his matches. He also continued to battle members of the nWo. In January, he faced Hall. This match again featured a cattle prod. Hall used it on Bill. This time, the prod did not affect him. Bill then used the prod on Hall and won the match.

In May, Sting once again had the World Championship belt. Bill wrestled him for the title. Both wrestlers were disqualified after other wrestlers entered the ring.

On October 24, Bill won the U.S. Championship again. He defeated Sid Eudy. Eudy wrestles as Sid Vicious. But Bill lost the title the next night to Bret Hart.

In December 1999, Bill and Hart were briefly the WCW Tag Team Champions. They lost the title on December 13 to Hall and Nash.

On December 20, Bill and Hart wrestled each other for the World Championship. Several members of the nWo came out to help Hart. They were Hall, Nash, Roddy Piper, and Jeff Jarrett. Bill could not defeat all of these wrestlers. He lost the match.

A Serious Injury

Bill wrestled again on December 23, 1999. He wanted to wrestle each member of the nWo. The last one left was Hart. But Hart left the ring before Bill could pin him. Bill became angry. He used his arm to smash the window of a car at the arena. He cut the tendons in his right arm. These thick bands of tissue join muscles to bones.

The injury was not the first of Bill's wrestling career. In October 1998, he suffered a head injury. In December 1998, he cut his head on the ringpost and needed 10 stitches.

Bill often wrestled members of the New World Order (nWo).

Bill was always able to keep wrestling after these injuries. But his arm injury was more serious. He needed 196 stitches to close the cut. He also had to stop wrestling for six months so that his arm could heal.

Chapter 5

Bill Goldberg Today

Bill returned to the ring in June 2000. The WCW had decided that Bill should be a heel. Bill agreed, even though it was hard for him. He knew that many children liked him. They saw him as a hero. Bill often visits sick children in hospitals. It would not be easy for him to meet these children if he became a heel.

On June 11, Bill went to the Great American Bash in Baltimore. He drove into the arena in a huge truck. He broke the rules and entered the ring during a match. Bill's first act as a heel

Bill returned to the ring in 2000 after his arm healed.

was to help Jeff Jarrett defeat Kevin Nash for the WCW World Championship.

Wrestlers often switch from being a babyface to a heel. They also can switch back again. Bill did not seem to like being a heel. He seemed ready to become a hero again. He also hoped to win another WCW World Championship.

Life Outside the Ring

Bill does not spend all of his time wrestling. He also has acted on TV shows and in movies. Bill appeared in the TV movie *The Jesse Ventura Story* and the TV show *Love Boat: The Next Wave*. In 1999, he appeared in a movie called *Universal Soldier: The Return*. The next year, he starred in a movie called *Ready to Rumble*. Bill plans to act in more movies in the future.

In 2000, Bill published his autobiography. Bill's brother Steve helped Bill write this book about his life. The book is called *I'm Next: The Strange Journey of America's Most Unlikely Superhero*. The book's title comes from Bill's

Bill did not seem to enjoy his new role as a heel.

winning streak. During that time, wrestling
fans would ask, "Who's next?" to wrestle Bill.

Bill has many other interests. He owns a
gym where people learn martial arts. These
arts teach people how to defend themselves.
Bill likes to fish and watch professional
hockey games. He also collects cars and rides
a motorcycle.

> After making a positive difference in a kid's life, it's difficult to go out there and do heel stuff.
> —Bill Goldberg, *World of Wrestling* magazine, 10/00

Helping Others

Bill has worked to help others since he became a wrestling star. He works with the Make-a-Wish Foundation. This group helps children who are seriously ill. Bill often visits the children to give them his autograph. He signs his name on a picture or a piece of paper. He also gives them tickets to his matches.

Bill is serious about his love of animals. His pets include cats, dogs, and horses. He also is a spokesperson for the Humane Society of the United States. Bill speaks about the society and how it helps animals. He made a TV commercial for the Humane Society. He also spoke to members of Congress about animal rights.

Bill Goldberg can seem mean in the ring. His job as a wrestler is violent. But he uses his fame to help people and animals throughout the world.

Bill often works with organizations that help children.

Career Highlights

1966—Bill is born December 27 in Oklahoma.

1984—Bill is named to the Oklahoma All-State high school football team and also is named the state's top defensive player.

1985–1989—Bill plays football for the University of Georgia.

1992–1994—Bill plays professional football for the Atlanta Falcons.

1995—Bill signs a contract with the WCW.

1997—Bill defeats Hugh Morrus to win his first official match.

1998—Bill wins the WCW U.S. and World Championships; *Professional Wrestling Illustrated* magazine names him Rookie of the Year.

1999—Bill wins his second U.S. Championship and teams with Bret Hart to win the WCW Tag Team title. He later suffers a severe arm injury and does not wrestle for almost six months.

2000—Bill returns to wrestling as a heel and publishes his autobiography.

Words to Know

autobiography (aw-toh-bye-OG-ruh-fee)—a book in which the author tells the story of his or her life

autograph (AW-tuh-graf)—a person's signature written on a piece of paper

disqualify (diss-KWOL-uh-fye)—to prevent someone from taking part in or winning an activity; athletes can be disqualified for breaking the rules of their sport.

mononucleosis (mon-oh-noo-klee-OH-siss)—an illness that causes weakness, fever, and a sore throat

opponent (uh-POH-nuhnt)—a person who competes against another person

rookie (RUK-ee)—a first-year athlete

scholarship (SKOL-ur-ship)—a grant of money that helps a student pay for education costs

signature move (SIG-nuh-chur MOOV)—the move for which a wrestler is best known; this move also is called a finishing move.

To Learn More

Alexander, Kyle. *Bill Goldberg.* Pro Wrestling
Legends. Philadelphia: Chelsea House,
2000.

Picarello, Robert. *Rulers of the Ring:
Wrestling's Hottest Superstars.* New York:
Berkeley Boulevard Books, 2000.

Teitelbaum, Michael. *Going for Goldberg!*
Dorling Kindersley Readers. New York: DK
Publishing, 2000.

Useful Addresses

Extreme Canadian Championship Wrestling
211 20701 Langley Bypass
Langley, BC V3A 5E8
Canada

World Championship Wrestling
1 CNN Center
Atlanta, GA 30348

Internet Sites

Canadian Pro Wrestling Hall of Fame
http://www.canoe.ca/SlamWrestling/
hallofame.html

Professional Wrestling Online Museum
http://www.wrestlingmuseum.com/home.html

World Championship Wrestling.com
http://www.wcw.com

Index